England's of the Mind

Nick Monks

Bluebell Publishing

For Amanda, Karl, Saskia

Acknowledgements: Sunk Island, Hull was published in Weyfarers, issue 114 and overlaid on a you tube video. Fulwood, Preston was published in Tearoom Books (South Africa) as an e book.

Title Page

England's of the Mind- Nick Monks

Published October 2018/By Bluebell Publishing
Printed by Lulu
www.lulu.com

ISBN: 978-0-9955203-6-3

Contents:

23) William Wilberforce
24) Keir Hardy
25) Lady Jane Grey

England's of the Mind

1

Sunk Island, Hull

1

I stand at the centre of an infinite plain satiated
Meadows forever swished, pollen scented air

The dark comes like a symphony of time
A body buffeted, leaning into the gale

My hood billows and crackles like an urban plastic bag
The night is a cathedral of stars and moon.

2

Once a city stood, then it fell into the clogged earth
Now this is all there is
Once there was a local pub, a train station, a semi
But now this is all there is
Once there was a marriage and kids
Until there was just this

City combing the elsewheres of nothing
The unseen river Humber's clogged swish.

3

Indecipherable something approaches
Through millennia and dark, breath bitten distance

Something that was always there in the soul the cranium

Something real, stone like tangible, but then gone forever
Leaving the dark, the gale, the vast sweep of river, a hollow
Sky- that whispers incantations.

Fulwood, Preston

2am, a park we held hands in, a road we walked down
The ruins of palaces and baroque symphonies

But for now- there is just the broken glass on the tarmac
A canal that winds somewhere closed half a century ago

The night life joy riders, the jiving strangers
Roads with clay and papier mache cars, granite institutions,
gone

Roads go to Blackpool, Blackburn, Chorley, Clitheroe, or here

Others- lives are not ours. Rotting laws and rules
Loves falling endlessly into stagnant ponds
Standing in the middle of proprietorship at last
Lorraine and I, others dream's behind closed curtains

We have outlived a cities nought. The brittle hush
Of finally alone, how many have achieved that.

Helvellyn

1

The grim terraced houses left behind like lead or anthracite
The stars that fall into a lake of ice love

The alarm clock mixed with milk bottles chink, and waste
refuge
The owls call broken at the foot of the sentinel hill

Crunched cans of lager on a midnight sofa
As the feathered heart of the car, has already left with us

Into the rocks of granite, where we climb higher
Above the wrecked castles, into our true worth.

2

There a map of peaks and fields, the Solway firth, the Irish
sea
Below shins, our elbows, fingers, toes, perused

Shivering in billowing kagools by the summit cairn
Catching the rain like a wilderness of a centuries thirst

Wishing to go higher still into what's possible
Above lingers like love, a grey motorway

Into the dark rooms like minds, a clock, a fridge hum
Aching limbs, granite rocks in the soul, the mouth.

11

Hampstead Heath

It's your day off from the
Macdonald's job on the Strand
So- from the shared room in Willesden Green
You jog east
You know you don't need a map
You will find the park as an eel a river

After fleet jogging over busy roads
Noticing autumn leaves falling
Thinking about the BA course
Your due to start in three weeks in Hull

You wish Hampstead Heath where bigger
Jog all directions, on each path there is.
Sit on the grass
See a depraved city's skyline of tumbling hope
Think I do not belong there, or here, or anywhere
The autumn leaves tumbling cascading, through a world.

New Forest

Helen and I, park the car
It's our one day in seven off work

We walk into the trees
Along the path, over heath
Through more trees
Helen holds out a hand and I ceremonially
Help her over marsh, abstract feminist though she is

We think we alight a quail
An explosion of small wings from tussock grass
Other birds, nuthatch/ lesser spotted woodpecker/
Coal tit/ tree creeper/ tree sparrow

In the pub in Beaulieu
We sip two half's of cider
The sun of march plays for the first time in the day

The mist over the heath is alluring
The day over. A car ride north. Back to work.

Dartmoor

You wanted to go here
But the DWP only give you £35 a week
So you hitch from Bristol
In the village of Rundlestone
You buy a can of coke
Edmund Spenser, Maya Angelou, Bertrand Russell
On your mind
The best books you can find in Bristol city library
With the exception of Edmund Spenser
None of which you would choose
You climb the high Rundlestone Tor
and North Hessary Tor, moors of Dartmoor
Write a poem on the summit
And sleep the night on a church bench in Rundlestone
In the morning you must hitch back
To your shared house where your
House mates are "up for" tyre theft
When you wake at 5.30am in dawn light
The church gate that was locked shut, is open.

The Wash

The grey sea becomes light blue, then at the horizon silver
Dunlin and knot curl then land with precision
The wind whips and buffets
Miles of grass fields and breaches
A light- yellow sun in a vast amphitheatre of sky

The three of you lie beneath the breach summit
Smoke roll ups
Against the winds bite

There over the tides ebb
Two hen harriers steal over the scattering waders
The sea comes in again, but we are gone
Just visitors in a hostile, brutal, enchanting north- sea saga.

Cairngorms

You cannot afford the youth hostel in Braemar
So- at dusk pitch a tent in a farmer's field
In the morning as you dissemble the tent
A storm sends it scattered into the sky like a kite

Through Caledonian fir trees- into Glen Dee
You've wrapped bin liners around you
Beneath your kagool
The rain sleets driving hard at your body
Through the Lairig Ghru Pass
A simple cross reads two names of the dead
Sheer sides of granite on either side
Walking rock to rock,
Tarrying in a seedy damp mountain hut shelter
Then after 18 miles and a further walk
Arriving in Aviemore and hitching south.

London

On a day when your not working
You catch a tube from Willesden Green
To London centre. Walk for seven hours
Through the business city, east
Finally you conclude there is nothing here
Just a ghost of a city, given over to pigeons
A city that can bite. But for now lets you wander
Return to your B and B room with ghost dust.

Hull

Wandering the city centre
Thinking of the sweat
The raw attrition of the sea
It takes months of studying
To see the beauty in the brown mud Humber
Not the silver of the Dordogne
Or the grey of the Severn
You are perturbed by the featureless
Rows of terraced houses
With straight streets
The bleak cold parks
The destitution, stillborn dreams
After 30 years in exile from Hull
Only the carefully teased out searing beauty
Of the Humber could draw you back
As long as you could sail away
On a rotting steel yacht
Back to Stavanger Norway
Away from the industrial estates
And the taste and smell of glue or fish
Into to the heave, the toil of the foretold north- sea.

Bristol

I do not come to work
To start a family, to study
I have wandered Hull/ London/
I come as a ghost
To walk each day through Clifton/ Bishopston/ Horfield
Southmead/ Bedminster/ Redcliffe/ Totterdown / Redland

Once again, I find nothing
Just poverty, injustice, corruption, augmentation
I come in the name of none
I found nothing notable or divine
In the daily walks
Not even a poem
I shed you off Bristol now, as I did then
A city of material pursuit
With the masses crawling and staggering
Sat at the back of the race
Penned in by barbed wire
And five thousand cathedrals in a botched building job.

Norwich

In the middle of East Anglia
A beautiful cathedral
A place perhaps were Plantagenet kings
Rode on horseback
Across the windswept fens

I have never been there! So- this poem is more real
Kerry and I drove from Cley marshes, Norfolk
Where we had been bird watching
Then saw nightjars at dusk in Thetford forest

We looked at the cathedral
A central focus for cities
Drank two double expressos each in a café
Walked down high street
Considered a hotel
But decided to drive in the light night traffic
Back to Warrington, where I have never lived but have visited
Because I have never been to Norwich-
This is the most real of these poems.

Liverpool

You once came working in care work
Traipsed around Albert dock
Got a cruise boat along the Mersey

But mostly you came to go to
Dead Good Poets Society
After the hilarious readings
On Northern Ireland sectarianism
Prostitution, getting drunk, other debauchery
You would drive around Liverpool
Entrapped by the one- way systems
As if the neon streets could impart something vital
Then away to the M6 and 90 mph north to Preston.

Manchester

After scores of youthful shopping for vinyl trips
This is your dream for Manchester
A vast botanical garden/ the new Alps to the north
More cosmopolitan than New York/ and higher and more
skyscrapers
An elevated mono rail network/ a desert/ a rainforest
adjoining/
Off the Flyde a vast coral reef bathosphere/ a superlative art
gallery/ An constructed fabricated arctic bathosphere

Still even without it jives
The accents are like yours
And even without the above adornments
You wonder at the vastness of architecture
Built on slum graves like Angel Meadow
Rising via cotton and coal. A conurbation urban maze
You wandering past Victorian dilapidated mills
Crossing the river Irk. Treading down Deansgate.

Salisbury

There are two second hand bookshops
Or where in Salisbury
Somehow when you come here to wander
And shop/ browse
You always find yourself inside the bookshops
Or admiring the cathedral

To get a good view
You walk along the River Avon
There a rarish water rail
Surprises amidst- mute swans, coots, moorhens, mallards
You watch the birds jerky stealth along the river bank

There in un- impended view across the fields
The Early English Gothic cathedrals grey sides
With a delicate sharp splinter of a spire
Which rises higher high into the adorning sky.

Houghton, Preston

In this room of magnolia walls
A cricket pitch at the back
The estate street at the front
I can envision all without going out
Hill house lane
With hedges screening farmer's fields
Where I have in the car's headlights seen
Deer, bats, hedgehogs, foxes, hare
The crescendo of hills rising that gives to
Blackburn or in the opposite direction Preston
Bamber bridge with an urban jive
Quirky niche shops- some shops can't
Make up their minds what they sell
The housing estate of streets
You've never had a reason to visit
In this room of magnolia walls
I do not need to go outside.

Cape Cornwall

The hotel is set back from the coast
A hotel like Manderley, or Graceland or a Welsh castle
You walk through the grey drizzle
Down slope to the ocean
On the rocky granite outcrop jutting out to sea
There are pebble beaches to the left and right
Gannet prevue the sea. Kittiwake and fulmars
fall from the cliff sides
to clamber the air on wings

You climb over the granite boulders
To the beach on the right side
Two seals heads poke from the water
The ocean bashes in against the granite

On the smooth circular pebbles
You a 12 year old gaze out into the
Grey/ light purple/ green Atlantic

In return the Atlantic throws- back rain gales
And segmented whipped waves
You toss a pebble into the sea.
Turn walk back to the ramshackle hotel of dreams.

St Just, Cornwall

Surrounded by the Atlantic washed fields
Bleak forlorn barren verdant
Far westerly town of tin and copper
The small town, in the name of celandine and meadow
Where Rhiannon lived
A girl with black hair and blue eyes
Who smeared lipstick all over her face
Then presented herself, to me

We picknick on the three ways refractured light of St Ives
At night bonfires on the hills celebrate
The Tuatha de Danu
Rhiannon is gone into indelible memory
I wander the painted houses streets of St Just
Stand in the square,
A forever quest for the princess of heath and moor.

Brighton

You've finished the 11am to 3.30pm shift
As a kitchen porter in Wheelies hotel
It is November and dark, your next shift starts at 10pm
You wander around Hove
The Walkman earphones tight in your ears
Listening to Elkie Brooks- Gasoline Alley
The Cure- A Forest, Thompson Twins- Storm on the Sea

Along high street, through the lanes
Along grand parade. Always the delicious black sea
calling you
Inevitably you find yourself by the promenade
But you do not tread out onto the pebble beach today

The gale is ferocious. So- you retreat inland
And back to the B and B room with a bag of chips for tea
Just one more circuit- "Into the trees. Into the Trees/ find a girl
while you can" "Sometimes I dream/ sounds all stay the
Same/ sometimes I dream, Charlotte sometimes"
You think: where next? Return to dress for the evening shift.

Birmingham

Your- with Musmoo
Who's from some exotic Pacific Island
You can't remember the name of
Or it could be that trip by coach
To the NEC to see Dire Straights
With college/school friends
But it isn't
Your early for the Kleeneze conference-
Two hours early

So- you wander around locally
Step along- side a canals tow path
You have never walked aimlessly as a prophet
Around Birmingham. Just Bristol, Hull and London
So- you head back to the conference centre
You know what is- Birmingham -
Messy life's in contrition- with bureaucratic corruption
You do not need to walk footsteps around Birmingham

In the conference. Its funny.
A man applies face make up to a woman
To demonstrate Kleeneze make up.
You have no intention of hawking catalogue's
Your just here out of interest
And as you weren't doing anything better today
Such as writing a poem or poems.

111

Boudicca

Celtic warrior who led a revolt against Romans in Britain in AD 60 or 61. Queen of the British Celtic Iceni. Motives-possibly flogged, and daughters raped. Or according Seneca loans called in, which were given to Britons.

Boudicca led the Iceni the Trinovantes and others in revolt. Destroyed Roman Camulodunum (Colchester) In AD 60 or 61. Then attacked Londinium (London) and Verulamium (St Albans). Is a British folk hero. Died shortly after the uprising. And after battle of Watling road at which she was defeated, by Romans led by Suetonius.

Boudicca leading the Iceni
To claim back the inheritance
Of the Celts, the druids, the Britons
To return, to rewrite history
The British Joan of Arc
Surrounded by the forlorn
A flag of magenta unfurled in an East Anglian gale
She has come valiant, with a sharp iron sword
A defiant unperturbed fiery gaze
To reclaim the land of the Iceni and Trinovantes
the Catuvellauni/ Dobunni/ Atrebates
To lead the tribes
Over the land of Pennines, ancient forests, Lake district
Chalk downs, plains, moors.

—

Rhiannon raven goddess confers
On military strategy with Lugh a Welsh god
Around Stonehenge. Druids utter incantations
On a land without roman taxes. As Rhiannon a blesses

—

In a hamlet in Norfolk at night
The Iceni stand and wait
Glifieu the leader, with men, women and children
Await the return of Reghan with news
News born on hen harrier wings
Galloping fast over the fens, at 3am
In the hamlet of huts, snow baubles meander
And the water rivers- sings.

He returns. "She is dead." "Shortly after loosing
The battle of Watling Street"
Against Romans led by Gaius Suetonius Paulinus
"We must subjugate to roman emperor"
There is a resigned flicker of recognition.
Then all return to sleep

—

Her arms rising. On a fleet horse
Rallying, transformative, angelic queen of the great Celts
The celandine, nightjar, lynx, wolfs
Of a land sleeping now. With imbued dreams becoming.

Richard 1, Coeur de Lion

8th September 1157 to 6 April 1199

King of England from 1189 until his death. Third of five sons of Henry 11 and Eleanor of Aquitaine. Also known as Occitan for reputation of terseness. And Richard the lion heart, as accomplished military leader and warrior.

Lived for long periods in France
Most of time was involved with the third crusade
Never won Jerusalem.
But won battles against Saladin
Spent time in captivity
Criticized for using kingdoms
To gain taxes for war
Possibly only ever in Britain for six months
Revered in both France and Britain
For his bravery in battle
Often referred to as Richard the lion heart
His brother John ruled (badly) while away on crusades.

King Richard brandishing the
Robust iron double edged sword
En- route to Jerusalem
To bring the chalice, to bear on his kingdom
A Knights Templars codes, chivalry- honour, courage, defend
the weak, spirituality, honour truth,
A prisoner on mainland Europe
A fire breathing lion,- Hamlet
In disguise, in cognito, wandering back to Amiens
Guinevere waiting in the tower of London

—

Childhood fables depict:
Saladin, cutting a ribbon in half with a sharp scimitar
Richard Coeur de lion, cutting a bar of iron in half
With large powerful sword-
His brother John, foe of Robin Hood

—

I imagine him in a dark roomed castle
His mind appealingly elsewhere from kinghood
Enjoying the wealth.
Perhaps his crusades saved him from courtly intrigue
Time slips from year to year
From battle to long march. A lame horse perhaps
Safe though from the fate of Richard 111.

Crows take off from the trees outside the castle window
Thousands of men must be enlisted
Though I know little. But scant legend
Perhaps his legacy is still entwined with today's eras.

William Wilberforce

24 August 1759 to 29 July 1833

1833 slavery abolition act. Born in Kingston on Hull
Became an evangelical Christian in 1785. Politician/
philanthropist. Lived in Kingston upon Hull. 1787,
became involved with a group of slave activists Charles
Middleton/ Hannah More/ Thomas Clarkson/ Granville
Sharpe.
Can be rightly criticised for underlying conservatism and
ignoring poverty in Britain. Died 3 days after 1833 act was
sure to be passed. Supported free Sierra Leonne.
Convinced of the importance of a religious moral
education. Against cruelty to animals.

The cobbled streets of
Princes Avenue/ Beverley Road/ Spring Bank/ Newlands
Avenue /Cottingham Road- a map wherein lies squalor and
destitution
Unremitted by green verdant Pearson Park/ West Park/East
Park
Anlaby Road- more disadvantage. Also- Priory Road
The workers factories of Sutton Fields Industrial Estate

One day William walks away from the centre of Hull
Away from the beautiful lure of the Humber
Along Spring Bank. Then Princess Street
By Newlands Avenue into Cottingham Road
There and around him poverty and destitution
Always the dirt embedded non- royal sweeping Humber

In a vast barren wide brown sweep
Heading out into the silver/light blue North- Sea
The city of rows of dingy poor houses
The flat fields of the East Riding
Reside like a rosary in his mind
The vast sky over the flat wilderness plain

Snow on Hull. The river a snow medley
Him a person predicated on the evangelical bible
Carrying his god unto Westminster
To enable the end of the triangular trade in slaves
While ignoring the squalor and destitution around him
Like the conservatives in the Britain of 2018.

Keir Hardie

15 Aug 1856 to 26 Sep 1915

Scottish socialist politician and trades unionist
Led labour party, first labour MP
Was a Georgist for a number of years (early 20th C
emphasis on tax on land)
Supported Scottish home rule and land restoration
Was a Fabian socialist (gradualist and reformist efforts in
democracies)
Won as an independent candidate West Ham South in
1892
Then helped to form labour party
Hardie was also a lay preacher
Supported women's suffrage (gained in Britain 1928)
Self- rule for India, and an end to segregation in South
Africa.

The countryside of Lanarkshire
To the east of the grime of Glasgow
Keir Hardy can see the injustice
That others choose to ignore
As he takes a Saturday hike over the heather
The red grouse taking off from Lanark moor

In 1892, proudly an MP. The first labour member
Founding a party. That would later deliver via Beveridge "the
welfare state" tackling disease/ want/ ignorance/ squalor/
idleness

Socialist aims:

No excuses,
The exploited workers to be given
Right to organize in trades unions
No excuses.
Free education, Karl Marx said
Paid work leave.
Universal franchise, as of a women's vote
A state on the side of citizens
The green of the moors becomes vivid greener
The dream of the whole man
As a Merlin sheets on golden wings over the slope
Free from alienation and servitude

In the pitch- black cramped tunnel
Digging the pick into the rich black seam
Learning shorthand in the evening at night- school

Redistribution of wealth.
A curlew's cascading tweets
As the bird lands in the reeds
The vivid figurine colours of a Lowry painting
Adequate housing.
No excuses- health care
No excuses
A living wage.

Keir Hardy became the first labour MP in 1892
Member- for West Ham South, initially won as an independent
Then with others, founding figure of the Independent Labour
Party in 1893.

Lady Jane Grey
1537 to 12 February 1554

Queen for nine days- 10 July 1553 to 19 July 1553
When Edward V1 lay dying, he nominated Jane Grey as heir
Partly as Mary his half- sister was Roman Catholic
And Jane Grey was Protestant
Third succession act: Mary and Elizabeth were declared illegitimate
The privy council supported Mary
Jane Grey awaited coronation in the Tower of London
Queen Mary planned to marry King Phillip of Spain
Jane Grey had an excellent humanist educationist
Reputation as one of most learned young women of day
Considered as a political victim and martyr
Both her and her husband were executed on 12 Feb, 1554.

Awaiting queen- ship
While others plotted
Swords is it
The ravens on the castle walls
Something ominous
Mary gathering armed men
Approaching the tower palace walls
Jane and her husband tried
For high treason in November 1553
Her father deserted her.

Jane Grey in prison
In the tower

Watching avidly the chink of light
In the corner of the cell
From the high bars.

The queen temporarily
That never was
Who perhaps would have been a great queen
Yet the world brutal, discerned otherwise.

A rightfully good queen
Educated, enlightened, well read
A perfumed ghost who left
Swords and treachery
To embrace the grave.

In the tower prison
Not the tower throne room
Chinks of light delectable
Jane is thirsty
If she could translate the ravens calls
Ravens even turned to nightingales
Her song for Britain. Deadened
A queen thirsty without water
Her etude forbidden to unfurl
Was she too pretty, too well read
Too beautiful. Too enchanted
Only the delectable chink of light
Now from high in the dark cell
A nightingale's song would be better
Than the cruel portent death
Silver blue light cascading like fresh clean-
Blue water and a song of the redstart
And mistle thrush. What do they talk about

In the state room concerning me
She enfolds the cape around her
The light cascading is just for her and divine.

Her husband Guilford Dudley was
Executed earlier in the day on tower hill
Lady Jane Grey watched the execution from a window.

She was dressed in black
She flirted with the executioner
Gave a speech in which she confessed sins
"Good people I am come hither to die, and by law I am
condemned to the same"
She keeps her reformist views- dies as a martyr- aged sixteen
Gave her handkerchief and gloves to Elizabeth Tilney
Took off her gown and headdress and collar
Put on blindfold and tossed her hair out of the way
Then panicked briefly as couldn't find the head block
Quipped as she took off her cloak
Was 16. Executioner beheaded her with one stroke
England didn't want an exemplary good queen.

48

www.ingramcontent.com/pod-product-compliance
Lightning Source LLC
Chambersburg PA
CBHW030306030426
42337CB00012B/602